Bouquet

Also by Harry Burrus

A Game of Rules (1989)
I Do Not Sleep With Strangers (1987)

BOUQUET

Poems
by

Harry Burrus

Black Tie Press
Houston

MCMLXXXIX

Design consultant and Black Tie logo by John Dunivent

Art & design work by Harry Burrus

Library of Congress Cataloging-in-Publication Data

Burrus, Harry, 1944-
Bouquet.

I. Title.
PS3552.U7643B68 1989 811'.54 88-63413
ISBN 0-941749-03-7 (cloth signed ed.)
ISBN 0-941749-05-3 (pbk. signed ed.)
ISBN 0-941749-07-X (limited ed.)

Manufactured in the United States of America

FIRST EDITION

for Morris and Eleanor Gabel

Harry Burrus at Corinth, Temple of Apollo

Contents

Foreword

The irony of a bouquet is that its beauty signals its end. Flowers, though lovely, pulled from the soil, their nourishment, begin to perish even before the last arranged gesture or setting. Love is no less ironic. Lovers taken in by the living color of their intimacy become irretrievably lost. They never develop roots, going instead for immediate, easy pleasure. A fragrance. A color. A flush here. Or there. The taste of shared wine. Moments of passion and undoubted words become a matter of being alone. As the romance fades, a lover leaves . . . time to meet someone else. It is a tribal progression, a rite of passage. Seeking, finding, losing, seeking.

We do not so much remember the exchanges, because words are just symbols, but we live with and within memory itself. The touching, but unable to let go of touch . . . promises floating on the thirst of a white, cold sea to islands which exist only as photographs, shared words caught in a powerful undertow.

"A voice distant from its speaker,
To be read as a page of memory,
A fiction for my imagination."

Inhale. Exhale. Rhythms change, fluctuate. Only the moment is precise. Because it was, but is no longer, and will not be. A birthday. A dark day. A bouquet.

"In this empty space,
The quiet amplifies the dark sounds and the only
Beam of stimulation is remembering you. I thought
I was a brave man. But I feel like a madman . . .

I wasn't even looking . . . for anyone at all.

Why am I alone?"

Questions and statements must be asked, even if the questions themselves lead us into our own defeat.

Reason for despair? As if we have been confronted by a house of closed doors? Not when there is still time to throw away the paper cup and catch the matinee. The theater, after all, is right next to the florist.

Loris Essary
Austin, February, 1989.

Bouquet

What is real one moment has become imaginary the next.
You believe what you see now, and the next second
you don't anymore.

- *Robert Frank*

Museum Piece

From the moment I first saw you
In Florence, I've wanted one like you,

One I could call my own. For years I kept
the idea of you while I developed my skills.

When I determined I was ready, you served
As my model, and, while the wheel spun,

I drew the revolving clay up with my thumbs
And fingers, drawing up your sides to the desired

Shape. Nature has not been my teacher.
I began by having less, at least not as much

As I saw in others, but I knew I would possess
And embrace you. Words would come later.

The firing took several days, three more
For the fires to die down, the kiln to cool

Before the opening. Many firings were required
For the hardening, for the glaze and abstraction

Of fused colors, before you could walk with or past
Your Maker, shaping all things to come.

Correspondence

After you read my letter,
I feared my intentions

Would not be grasped
And you would not understand.

Your interpretation does not console;
It is contrary to our agreement.

Last night, I dreamed you forgave
Me and pillowed on my arm.

I can tell by your reaction
My words were inadequate,

I was wrong to rent them,
Hoping they would curve you

Back to me, into our pearl light.
I can't explain the tempest;

I should have come to see you myself
To demonstrate how strong we are,

Showing that our minds' excessive anguish
Was really over nothing.

Song

Every two hours or so, to break the monotony,
I pull off into one of those scenic turn offs,
I walk around, stretch, and pour a coffee from my thermos.
I like looking into the distance, following the horizon,
to see how far I've come and to measure where I am going.
No matter which direction I face, I see you walking
out of mesquite, from behind green hills, or emerging
from a long stretch of bluebonnets. A half hour ago,
your face rested on the horizon line like a sun setting
or the moon slowly rising. This love of you is before me,
always, and in all directions.

Agreement

I don't want
from you

what others
have had

or what you
have given them.

I offer you
my visions,

my humor, and
a willingness

to always go
for ice cream.

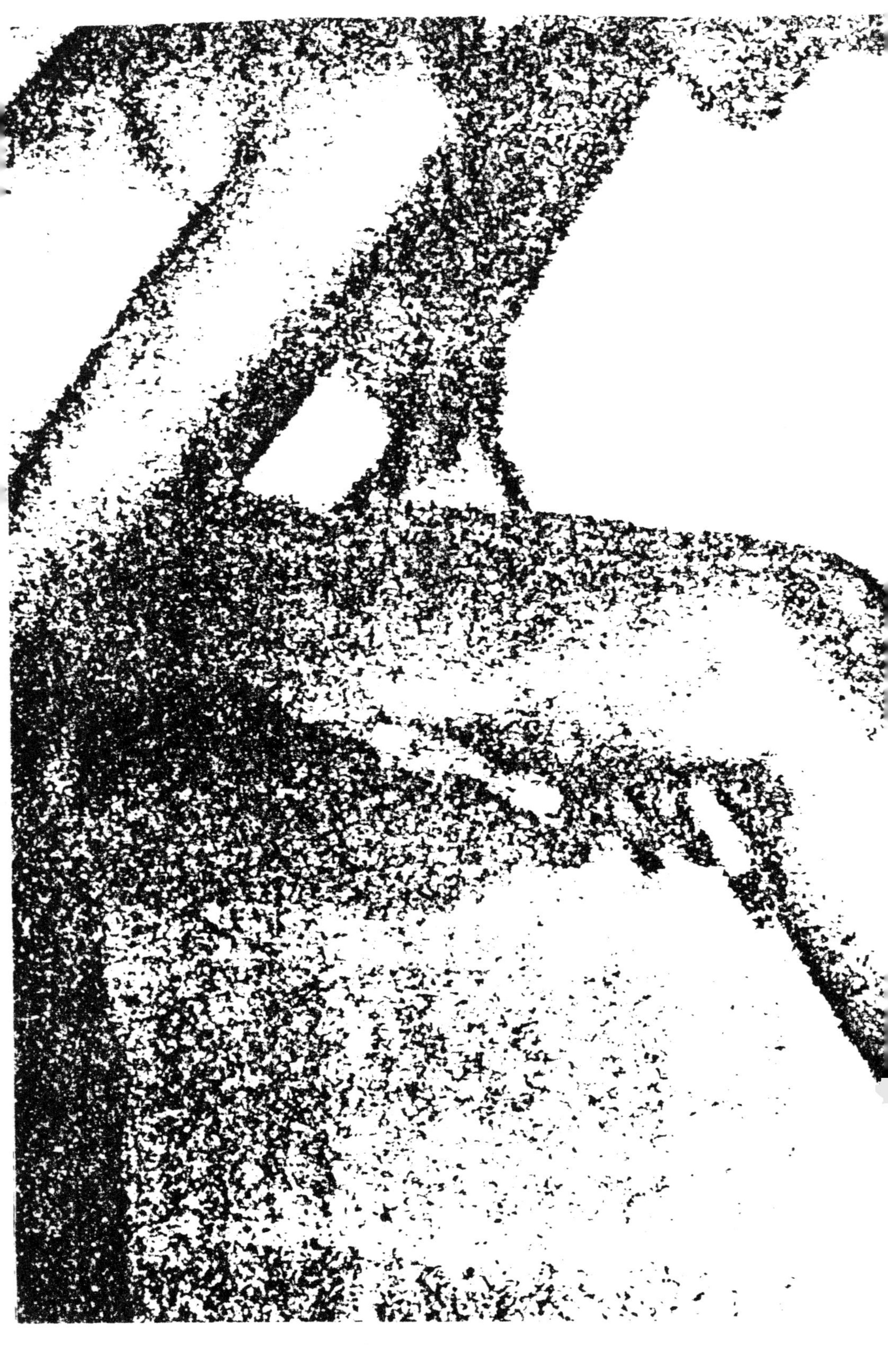

Bargain

Staying out late every night.
Drinking for pleasure and for the sake of it.
Refusing to go home, to spend time with her.
Refusing to believe I wasn't being me.
Getting into the bar scene, using my hands,
The rest of my body.

Finding women easy, but not remembering
The next day. Refusing to think it would end,
That darkness meant something besides night.
Finding you was another word for living.
Deciding to jettison the blackout recollections.
Deciding to drink only of your nectar.

Offering

There were no direct moves on your part.
You didn't approach me the standard way,

By using corny lines or adopting a come hither look.
I knew right away there was much we could share.

What I'm saying may puzzle you, since, you don't know me,
But I'm convinced we are a treasure.

We are of the blue ground, a flawless diamond,
Only to be cut and polished. It is up to you.

I've come to you because your fine brilliance
Etched itself deeply, reaching my center,

Captivating me. I was unable to turn away,
And didn't want to. Many couples speak, but say little,

Their words caught in a powerful undertow.
They are unable to save themselves. Your image dances,

Moving in fifty-eight facets, a sun
Casting no shadows. I see you clearly,

A magnetic force pulling and pushing me to you.
I like the way you move, cutting and giving shape

To space. I like the way you carry yourself,
Shoulders back, confident, and strong . . .

Together we will uncover ancient markings
And, with one of our edges, carve our name.

We have not discussed the obvious and I appreciate that.
Your eyes tell me we know many secrets.

What we have is rare.
Do not be frightened by this precious gem.

Souvenir

I meant to
send you a bud

from the Pin Oak
outside my window,

but
I knew

you wouldn't
want me

to sever the branch.

Koutoubia from Her Window

I spent each evening with her
That winter in Marrakech, remaining
In the medina until the early morning
Light painted the city red. Her room
Bled with saffron, lemon, and coriander.
She kept the shutters open, letting in
The Grand Atlas mountains, the minaret,
And the wailing echo of the muezzins.
She wore a hooded cloak, kopal necklace,
And veil. After a dinner of couscous or tagin,
We'd rinse our hands and drink mint tea.
In order to understand her better and for her
To trust me, I held her at a distance, knowing
All night moves were in the hands of Allah.

Invitation

Come visit me sometime
When you are alone

Or want to talk to someone
Who will listen.

I won't offer you my shoulder;
You shouldn't lean on anything.

Talking may ease your burden
And encourage you to walk erect.

You have no reason to be stoop-shouldered;
Your body houses many treasures -

When you stop by
We'll discuss some of them.

It Happens

I know the caper.
I've been there,
the "not wanting to be with
the one you're with"
or actually looking
for someone
to be with - scene.

I'm not there anymore,
(I'm pleased to say).
And, when it happened to me,
I wasn't even looking
for action,
for anyone at all.
Really.

I'm not the type
for meat marketing.

But, let me tell you,
it happens.
It happened to me,
indirectly,
and I'm glad.
You never know
about this kind of thing.
It's not something
you can plan. And,
if you want my advice,
just let the pace
(or whomever)
establish itself.
Then allow it to continue.
In fact . . . encourage it.

About Face

In a lifetime, a face faces a legion of faces
And rarely do we show our noble face,

The beautiful fresco we consider the principled
Likeness. Which one should I show you?

Which one can I show? Situations such as this
Always depend upon the circumstance. What

Kind of moment are we having, need I ask?
How often do you show yours, your unlayered look?

Sometimes, one face reveals another, another
Layer, previously undiscovered; sometimes the other

Face reveals one's own. And if this should happen,
We are making progress. By removing the veil,

You have revealed my unfeigned face and I will
Relinquish it, only to you. This, indeed,

Is another look, a sincere one, unlike the others.
There is a look for every look, a face for every

Face, regardless which one you wear. And wearing
A different look helps one to understand one's own.

I'm wearing your face most of the time; I've
Grown to love it. Besides, I like the look.

Absurd Hour

Midway in the cluttered room or facing
The crevice where the walls touch, I am alone.
The door confronting the outside light is open,

But only darkness snakes its way through.
I find myself isolated, the separation not from
Any action I have launched. In this empty space,

The quiet amplifies the dark sounds and the only
Beam of stimulation is remembering you. I thought
I was a brave man. But, I feel like a madman,

Fearful of emptiness. Why am I alone? What have I
Done to have to ask, what is it that tortures me?
I use to pretend I was higher, on the pedestal

Of some paradise . . . that we loved in a country
Beyond dreaming. Will all my longing, all of my love,
Make a difference? I am a corpse placed in an open

Coffin, a ship caught in the doldrums waiting
for a breeze to infuse motion back into its body.
Is this lifeless space my life without you, my life

With love drained from it, our light extinguished?
This can't be happening. Has this frightening, absurd
Event occurred . . . or is my imagination playing

Sorcerer, casting a warning, underscoring the meaning
Of appreciation, demonstrating the penalty for self-
Indulgence? Am I left only to see you in dreams,

Never to touch your face? When and how will I know?

Speaking Chinese

Late evening
Early morning

Broad smiles
Talking eyes

Two half moons
A full moon -

My hands grasping.

Asking for You

When I look into your eyes

I can hear your heart speaking.
The beat conveys warmth and affection.

When I take you in my arms,
Our kiss seals the appreciation.

In the questionable distance,
Waves merge with the sky.

Paroled

You have broken my self-imposed isolation.
And I am grateful for that. In my emotionally barren
Cell, I finally realized the magnitude of my naiveté,
The selfish motivation behind my thirst for experiences.

I was gullible about success, I was ridiculous
With my self-inflicted bruises and the many wounds
I put upon others. Only now is this disappearing.
Your kindness released long buried feelings, almost

Forgotten, but reserved for someone special, you.
Now pardoned, I know my guilt: living life as a fairy tale.
My re-evaluated beliefs can be shared without fearing
Incarceration. At last, I'm more mature, no longer

An emotional cripple. I'm better equipped to interpret
The fluctuations of my changing rhythms. With you
By my side, I can embrace each morning, look forward
To tomorrow and feel good along the way.

Courvoisier

I've lived with the desire to grow old
With one woman, somehow knowing I'd lose
The one I wanted most. She had the beauty
Of a French movie star, a Catherine Deneuve
Or an Anouk Aimée. The bed is as we left it,
An abandoned camp fire, cold as the indifferent sea,
Disheveled with waves of books and bottles,
But most of all - her smell,
Which is like the sun going down. I can't bear
To imagine her being touched by someone else.
Her lips giving another man a chance to discover . . .
The candle on the table extends its reach,
Writhing over the wall, in sync with the storm.
She loved moving in the rain, her skin glistening,
In and out of imagined spaces. Always the rain . . .
Forming an endless backdrop to my saturated senses.
We had great zing, gulping down the happiness.
I loved when she tossed salad, brown hair loose,
Hanging past her shoulders. Wearing only that smile.

Anniversary

My outstretched leg
leaves the warmth of the covers

and braves the morning cold,
but you are not here.

The smell of coffee
and bacon enters the room.

I'll pretend I'm still asleep.
How nice, you remembered

our special day.
Breakfast in bed will be fun.

Yearbook

You will probably be shocked
At anything I say
Or think it is a big lie -

Since things I have said to you

In the past six months
Have been anything but nice.
I really think you are a wonderful

Person and I can't thank you enough

For taking care of me this year.
We've had so many wonderful times
And I assure you I shall never forget them.

Especially October and November.   I know

There are numerous things
That you have heard,
But they aren't true.

In fact, a certain thing

That I said was for your benefit!
I will think of you next year . . .
Good luck with your studies . . .

And never forget that you can

Have any person on this earth -
Boy, aren't you thankful
You don't have me!

Please take care of yourself

And, if you can spare the wishes,
Write me and tell me
What you are doing.

Have a happy birthday!

Empty Morning

Today, I flavor
My coffee with tears.

You were unfair
To leave me

Without a warning,
Without a kiss.

Finding you gone
And cold sheets

As a momento
Made getting up

Even harder.
It's so unlike you

To leave me alone
To embrace the new day.

The Guide

It's gratifying talking to you,

Listening to you speak of places
You've been, where you're going.
I wonder if I will ever leave.

I grieve about my past; I hope
My life will change. Never
Leaving home closes me in,

Not open as you are open. I strive
To alter my awareness by reading,
Listening, observing you, growing

With you as you grow. Trouble stirs.
My stomach churns; I fear you
Will leave, my exit to the other side

Then closed. I'll remain locked,
Confined by my surroundings, a cocoon
Waiting for the precise moment.

Mexico Was Months Ago

Darkness fills the empty spaces,
Seeking its own level.
I think too much.
Sitting here mindlessly,

I peel the wallpaper
Like the time your back got burned,
And I changed your skin with one hand.
I've been drinking since early

Afternoon, losing clarity,
You are a puzzlement . . .
If I could be with you now,
It would soften my confusion,

It would generate more light.
It's cold here.
To please you would take more than words.
Mexico's an apparition,

The swept-up dust of memory.
Walking the beach
That first gringo morning
Revealed a naked, sunning female.

I stopped five feet from her and stared.
You lit your eyes, igniting my foundation,
Your look undressed me . . . slowly
You turned over. I refused to blink.

You were casual and up front.
I was self-conscious, shy.

Over drinks at the hotel bar,
I somehow knew we were celebrating

Something that few people find.
Your flower opened in my heart
And the fragrance born from the blossoming
Allowed me to breathe for the first time.

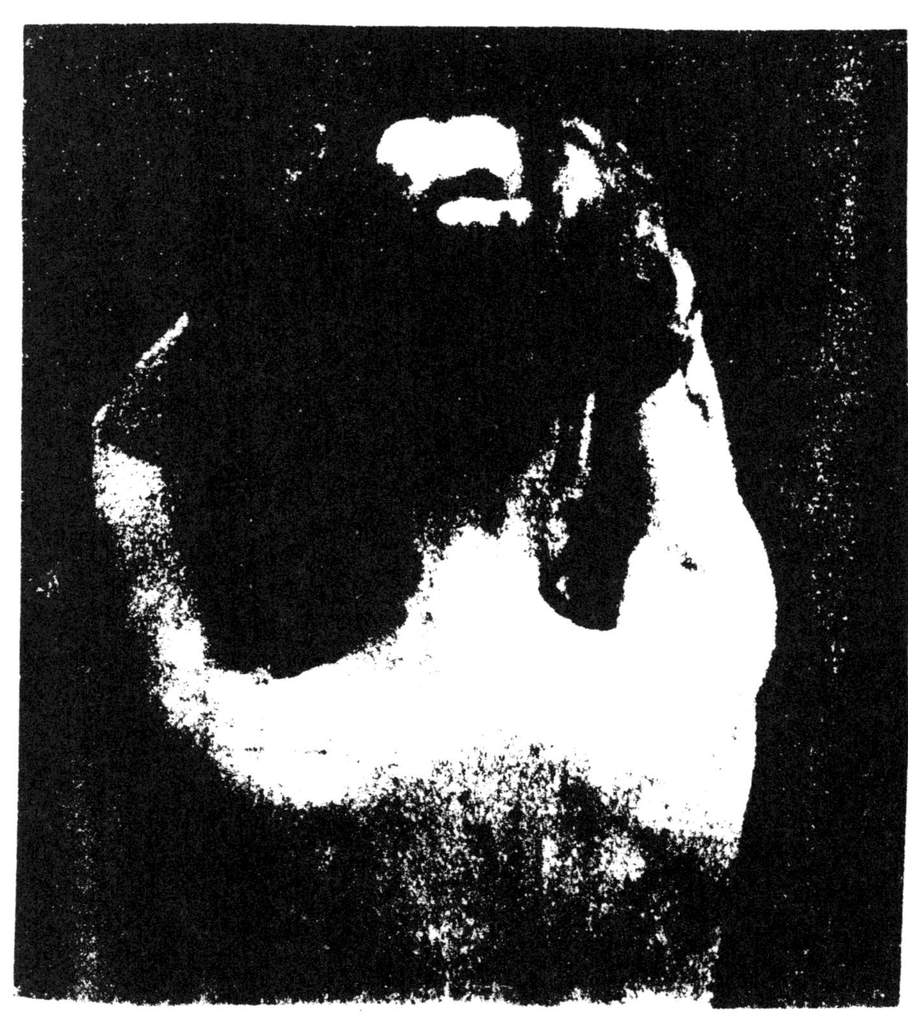

Daybreak

The morning
light peels away the darkness -
Our eyes refuel each other. Yesterday,
you were unhappy, thinking I no longer
cared for you. You were foolish
to worry. We will share many
fine moments. Today
is one of
them.

Skin Deep

Bananas
are fun
to
un
dress

Peeling
off
your things
is
better

I
like
natural
fruit
flavor

Beaux Mots

Why do I speak to you? You don't pretend to listen.
Do you really care? Words, after all, are just symbols
Used to reflect a meaning, thrown away like paper cups.

Why do you frame your lips? What are you saying
And to whom? Can you pick up my moves; are they obvious
Or subtle? Has any of this been said to you before?

Have you said something like this to someone else?
What do you expect? How do you translate our exchange?
Have you been fulfilled, satisfied, denied? Do these

Last three words apply? Please, be candid. I feel
A growing kinship with you, a bond; what does it mean?
What can it provide? Do you, also, wish for something

Grand? The seed exists, life is full of choices.
The muse of you has been with me for some time. Not always.
But often. Perhaps the idea of you planted the seed

Which has germinated. Is doubt growing? I am not vexed;
I want change. After all, I represent change for you.
I don't want you to change, though, aside from normal

Development. I'm still becoming myself. Are you searching?
Do you want to explore? To feel the wind, the sun, and
The waves? What do former lovers mean to you? You to them?

You have outgrown their reach. Now is our time for the sunset
Bell to vibrate through the cathedral, as we climb, clutching
Our passion, to our white, white tower, scattering stars.

Navigation

Your presence releases emotion
Which meanders like multiple rivers
Through my mind. This motion,

This somersaulting sensation,
Propelled by your growing, flowing
Attraction, stimulates me, sometimes

Unconsciously, to engage new tributaries,
To round other bends, seeking obstacles
And overcoming them. Is this force,

This warm glowing, mutual?
Are you also encountering foreign channels,
Experiencing rich deltas, looking

For the open sea? This sharing,
Living time with you intrigues me,
Enlists me, encourages me. We are

Assigned mates on a long journey,
A voyage to charter the uncharted.

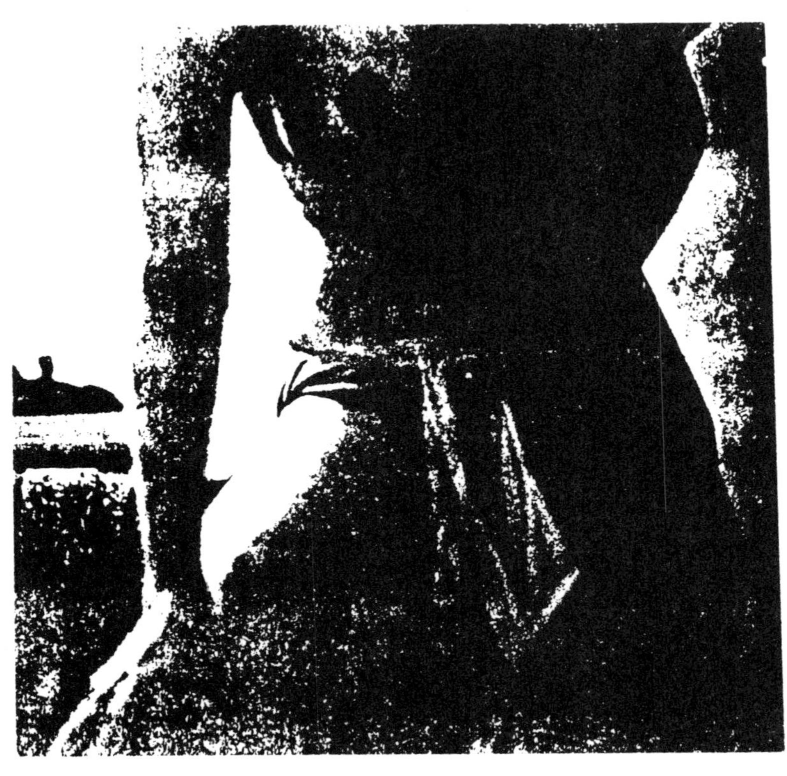

Thief of Hearts

The fragrance drifts past,
Tantalizing available appetites -
Volunteers prove plentiful.

The hungry are always wanton
And never out of season.
Eyes close, dizziness

In the perfumed air.
The love struck keep one thought:
Not of time or place, but to embrace

What's passing, unaware
Of their habit, giving of themselves,
Completely.   Soon feverish

And losing their saturated colors
And unable to distinguish
One bouquet from another,

Their strength languishes . . .
But nothing comes of nothing
And the thief moves on,

Singing a song so nostalgic and medieval.

Eye Within

How comfortable and safe sitting here in my little box alone, untainted, and unaware.
would — of
it — the
be — thrills
if — and
I'd — beauties
step — awaiting
outside — me
my — externally.
box? — I
I — remain
might — coiled
get — within
hurt, — my
I — imagination
don't — searching,
want — but
that — not
to — gaining,
happen, something happen! I can't bear these walls depriving me of my rightful knowledge.

Departure

He left the room
Without looking back,
Without saying goodbye.

Why do people leave pretending
They are not hurting, too?
It's time to meet someone else.

He left the door wide open,
Someone could walk in.
Maybe I'll go out, look around,

Check the scene, so to speak.

I'll Send for You

The white sand
on and on,
lit by a sliver of a moon.
The violet Pacific
pounding.
She, in her sweat
soaked hammock,
naked
as the eroded cliff
below,
bites into a dream
she clings
to:
Their first home,
built of plaited bamboo
and thatched
with woven leaves
of coconut palms.
She learned about
possessing
by being
possessed;
she cannot
remove him
from her body.
Their first
meeting
he handed her
shells
marked
with the names
of islands

he wanted
to photograph:
Easter, Pitcairn,
Fatu Hiva . . .
When she walks
the beach
and looks
far past
the blue,
she imagines,
before falling
asleep,
that they lie
and inhale
the exhalation
of surrounding forest,
mouth to mouth
with the breathing
greenery,
one
inhaling
what the other
expires.
Her life,
exploration,
and discovery.

Just one
believes
the promise.

Criterion

A closed door confronts me,

And then it slowly,
Gradually opens.
Why does this movement occur?
To encourage me to step forward

And look inside?
Is this act an introduction,
An invitation to a beginning,

A singular opportunity for our exchange?
What can be found in this well lit room?
The same that I encountered in the others?

Or will it be something unusual -
A chorus of orchids, blooming,
Or something spontaneous,

A roman candle
pin-pointing the Big Dipper?
I have seen those

Who refer to themselves as *Mystery* . . .
And I have aligned scores of the little pieces,
But my question lingers.

Does every meeting denote a puzzle
To be analyzed and taken apart
Before the sections can embrace,

Producing a phase called love?

Being with You

What I want
I know

What will I have?
I know not

Not knowing
What I will have

I will not
The unknown

A Hymm to Beauty

Deprived of its colored cloak

The slender, pronged staff
Shivers stoically in the breeze,

Though naked, its presence is austere,
Time renders the elements

Of erectness, of bending.
Beauty blossoms with the cold,

The warm, and variations of the two.
But, if like the evergreen,

Only one mantle is worn,
Beauty would not be discerned.

Passion

Slowly this defeat.
I can't believe
the amount of time
I spend thinking
about hot summer
nights when you
cared for me.
I hate the dark,
winter afternoons,

the cold streets,
and my single body.
There are no substitutes
for August,
our wetness.
You haven't written.
I often wonder
what you are doing -
my long legged beauty
who walked away -
I want you to know
I tried to care.

A Drink with You

Looking, talking . . . getting looks,
Hearing small bites of conversation,
Tasteless words . . . difficult chewing.

Sitting across from you, I drink you in
On an empty stomach, but the effect
Is heightened. Your eyes speak to me

In changing colors as they link with mine.
I answer questions I pose, many questions
That your eyes ask. Questions you must ask,

Since you are being prompted, though not
In a theatrical sense. You know the lines.
Don't worry. Delivery isn't important,

No one will upstage you. Much idleness is washed away,
No dust gathers. Your gaze carries me to many shores,
White beaches. Your eyes pull me across the hot sand,

In the coconut grove, we continue our discussion.
I answer your questions and go over and
Under your lines. You're my favorite one-act

Play. The sun feels good on the back.
A drink with you provides unlimited travel.
"Miss, another round, please."

Diary

We meet as usual at the Family Café
To share our early morning poems.
The children are in school, my husband's
At work, his wife is home,
  as I should be.
I look forward to this second
Cup of coffee. Temporarily,
I'm outside of an edgeless day.
His eyes look tired, but that smile
Reveals his joy to see me. I hope
My Clorox hands go unnoticed. They don't.
He holds them tightly. I know
He must leave; office hours beckon.
We take our final sips,
The good-bye kiss . . . until tomorrow.

Voyeur

Round, bizarre moon,
suspended above me,
   a cyclops
   seeing all,
except when looking
the other way.

You, too,
are surrounded by others,
yet remain alone.

What do you do
when you turn your back?
Watch something else?

It's hard to imagine,
you, who rule
the waves,
hang there, watching -

without ever intending to act.

Le Sort de l'Ombre

Intriguing shadow lingering before me,
Why can't you subdue your spiritual unrest?
Seemingly, you transmit sincere thoughts,
But these conceptions splash against the rocks,
Only to return again.
The tide must repeat itself.
But not you.
You can create
And seduce new forms
Without
Transcending
Into
A
Monotonous
Existence.
I ponder your refractive forms,
Yet, all shadows enrapture my soul.
Dancing before me, your flames
Are in the apex of my lens.
A shadow is misty from birth.
To what power shall I adjust my vision?
Shall I focus, at all?
Mythical Being,
Can you become master
Of your venomous existence?
At times, your images are poetic
And ascend the banal,
Only to
Diminish
Once
More.

Looking Forward to May

The first warm breeze
Carries images to thaw

Hibernated feelings.
Unfortunately, winds change

Direction. I am a victim
Of fair weather thinking, unless

I remain bear like and wait for you,
Our spirit glowing beneath the surface of caves.

Birthday

After many false starts,
The candles close their eyes.
Mouths are busy devouring

Headless shrimp, lump crab meat,
Oysters, medium rare roast beef,
And mounds of black fish eggs.

They all pretend to enjoy
Themselves. You bring me
Champagne. Your breasts deny

The wind. I want to bite them.
I try not to stare. The falling
Light has a sense of purpose,

A movement all its own.
I consider winking or showing
My teeth. You turn left,

Leaving behind orange blossoms
And the hint of a kiss
For my memory bottle.

Vertigo

I wonder, if my mind creates such dizziness now, future heights shall swirl the ground below me.
would I
have continue
you engaging
deeply you,
inhale making
this plans?
fragrant Yes!
air even
of one
delight, ecstatic delight . . . winds, don't rob me of that first embrace.
allowing
our
flower
to
blossom.

Renewal

It has been four days
Since you shared my bed.
I have seen night change colors

And I have breathed smells I never knew
Existed. None of which reminds me
Of you, only you are missing and I

Am alone, floating on a white, cold sea.
Each evening, the silence of the room
And empty bed closes in around my

Every movement, around every thought
I shape like stale air. Why did you
Deflect the tenderness and fade,

A voice distant from its speaker,
To be read as a page of memory,
A fiction for my imagination;

Why are you doing this to me?

Waiting to Be Picked Up

A river, a mirror,
Races in front of me.
The water is clear,
Too clear,
Leading me to believe
I can see beneath
The surface. I see
Myself, moving.
Going where?
Perhaps, it is unwise
To wish everything
Explained. But
Where does love go?
Emotions flow
Inside my head,
Less clear, but moving
As fast.
Going where?
I don't know.
It remains a mystery
Adding enticement
To the pursuit -
There is no trifling
With nature.
My thoughts are broken
Twigs,
Carried along,
Waiting to be
Picked up.
I hope I'm not
Alone,
Come autumn.

Once More

Real love
Doesn't die.

It may disappear,
Perhaps
Even be forgotten,
But,
It is always there,

Residing
Somewhere in the heart,
Locked in the soul . . .
To be remembered,

Waiting
To be born once more.

Imaginary Life

She would rather be on her own,
Traveling, using room service, and living
In cities where she doesn't speak the language.
Now, married into money, she faces the likelihood

Of bearing children and a good chance
She'll become a responsible, mature person;
For sure, she's made a commitment.
She wishes she could start over

With all of the mistakes erased.
If only she could go back. Back
To the labyrinth, where she saw no endings,
Where goals were not imagined,

When she didn't feel guilty about being
Happy, when every moment, every touch
Tingled with awakening, riveting
Her with excitement, and beauty could

Be seen anywhere. That was a time
When everything was as she wanted it to be.
There were no known answers and excess
Was something she didn't measure.

Disenchantment with friends, lovers,
Career, or marriage was not even a consideration.
She wished she could re-thread
Those strands of autonomy, but she knows

Far more than she cares to about living.
And, even though she remembers being taught,

"Everything remains a part of you,"
She no longer values that kind of information.

Living has become a sacrifice, a serious
Business of lies intertwined with other lives.
Beauty is a value accessible only
Through imagination, only by negating

The world and its primary structures.
She recognizes it's stupid
To confuse the moral with the aesthetic,
Besides, there's still time to catch the matinee.

Photo credit: Megan Gabel

Like a prism, Harry Burrus' levels and perceptions are multiple: the innovative, serious writer (M.F.A); the suggestive, dramatic photographer (M.A. Film); the provocative conversationalist and speaker (M.A. Speech & Dramatic Arts); the graceful, skillful tennis professional (All-American); the voracious traveler (since Denver, 1944). Burrus, a chameleon, lives with his wife, Megan, an attorney, in Houston, Texas.

This First Edition of Bouquet *by Harry Burrus (photographs & design by the author), Foreword by Loris Essary, set in Goudy Old Style and printed by Stuart McCarty at his Geryon Press, Limited, nineteen hundred and ninety, for and under the direction of Peter Gravis and Black Tie Press, Houston, Texas - art & design supervision by John Dunivent - is strictly limited to 250 copies on Mohawk 80 lb. White Eggshell; 200 in paper wrappers numbered & signed by the author; fifty copies are bound in cloth over boards, numbered & signed, of which the first six contain three prints by the poet, 20 copies are lettered G–Z, each supplemented by an original signed print by the author.*